Storyfun

for Flyers

Student's Book

Karen Saxby

CAMBRIDGE
UNIVERSITY PRESS

CAMBRIDGE
UNIVERSITY PRESS

University Printing House, Cambridge CB2 8BS, United Kingdom

Cambridge University Press is part of the University of Cambridge.

It furthers the University's mission by disseminating knowledge in the pursuit of
education, learning and research at the highest international levels of excellence.

www.cambridge.org
Information on this title: www.cambridge.org/9780521134101

© Cambridge University Press 2011

This publication is in copyright. Subject to statutory exception
and to the provisions of relevant collective licensing agreements,
no reproduction of any part may take place without the written
permission of Cambridge University Press.

First published 2011
7th printing 2013

Printed in the United Kingdom by Latimer Trend

A catalogue record for this publication is available from the British Library

ISBN 978-0-521-13410-1 Student's Book
ISBN 978-0-521-12667-0 Teacher's Book with Audio CDs (2)

Cambridge University Press has no responsibility for the persistence or accuracy
of URLs for external or third-party internet websites referred to in this publication,
and does not guarantee that any content on such websites is, or will remain,
accurate or appropriate. Information regarding prices, travel timetables and other
factual information given in this work is correct at the time of first printing but
Cambridge University Press does not guarantee the accuracy of such information
thereafter.

Contents

Ben's wishes

I have an uncle who writes books for children. I didn't see my uncle very often when I was a child because he lived in Africa, but he came to see us sometimes. When he did visit us, he usually told me one of his stories. I loved them all but 'Ben's wishes' was my favourite. My uncle told it to me one winter when it was very cold outside. I was about ten, I think.

A boy called Ben had two older brothers. The older boys often felt hungry and often got angry because they were so poor.

'Go and work in the fields!' they said to Ben each morning. 'Dig up some vegetables! Make us some soup for dinner!'

Ben always answered in the same way. 'But I want to go to school and learn all about the world!' The brothers just laughed and said, 'Don't be silly! You aren't clever enough to go to school like us.'

So Ben didn't go anywhere. He just worked in the fields in the rain, digging and planting, and planting and digging.

One very cold morning, Ben was planting some onions when he saw an old silver cup on the ground. He picked it up, sat down under a tree and cleaned it with his scarf. Then, very carefully, he put it down on the grass next to his bag.

Ben was tired and wanted something to eat, but he only had one small sandwich in his bag. He took it out, looked at the cup and said, 'I'm lucky to have this sandwich, but I'd like a lovely warm drink!'

Suddenly, the silver cup was full of hot chocolate. Ben was very surprised! He drank it all, but he still felt cold. He looked down at his old jacket and at the cup again and said, 'I'm lucky to have a jacket, but there are hundreds of holes in it. I wish ... I wish ... I could have a new coat!'

A beautiful coat made of wool suddenly appeared from somewhere in the sky. Now Ben was really surprised! He put it on. It felt soft and warm.

Then he opened a small book that belonged to one of his brothers. Ben looked at the cup one more time and said, 'I'm lucky to have this book with me today, but I'd like 100 new books so I can learn all about the world, please.'

Suddenly, 100 new books fell from between the leaves in the tree above him. Ben couldn't believe it! He felt so lucky!

He laughed and laughed, put the old cup in his pocket, carried the books home, sat down by the fire and read them all.

When Ben's older brothers came home, they were really angry. 'Where's our dinner? Where's our vegetable soup?' they shouted.

Ben looked up and said, 'I found an old cup in the field today. I think it understands about wishes. It gave me hot chocolate, a warm coat and 100 new books to read. I've learned all about the world and all the animals that live in our world too. If you want your dinner, just ask the silver cup for it!'

The two older brothers looked at Ben's new coat, his new books and the silver cup on the table. One of them picked it up. He got very angry. 'We have a wish too! Give us our dinner! We want it this minute!' he said.

The empty bowls were suddenly full of vegetable soup. The brothers couldn't believe it!

'Cup!' the oldest brother shouted. 'Give me a room full of money.'

'Give me more money than my brother and a room full of sweets,' the other brother said.

Suddenly, there were sweets and money everywhere. The brothers began to fight.

'Give me that cup!' one shouted.

'No!' the other one said. 'It's mine. It's not yours. Give it to me!'

The cup fell on the ground and broke, and all the sweets, the money, the vegetable soup, Ben's warm coat and his 100 new books disappeared.

They were nowhere in the house.

I felt very sad when my uncle told me that part of the story. But then he added, 'But the cup couldn't make all the stories about the world disappear from Ben's head. And when Ben was a man, he visited all the countries in the world and wrote lots of stories about the animals and people who lived there to tell to children.'

I never knew my uncle's first name. I just called him Uncle.

Perhaps, just perhaps, it was Ben.

Ben's wishes

A New words for you!

Draw lines between the green words and the pictures.

There's a hole in my sock!

Wow! She's lucky!

He likes digging!

Stop fighting!

B Right or wrong?

Tick the right or wrong box.

	right	wrong
Example: The girl heard this story in the summer.	☐	✔
1 The story was about three brothers.	☐	☐
2 Ben was the youngest brother.	☐	☐
3 Ben's brothers were kind to him.	☐	☐
4 The cup that Ben found was made of gold.	☐	☐
5 Ben looked for the new books in the tree.	☐	☐
6 The cup broke when it fell on the floor.	☐	☐

C Who's talking about this story?

Tick the right box.

A
☐
I liked it because the brothers are funny. My favourite part was when Ben went shopping.

B
☐
I liked it when Ben's books fell out of the tree. I didn't like it when the brothers got angry.

C
☐
The brothers were lucky because they lived on a farm. I liked it when Ben cooked the onion soup for dinner.

Do some colouring and drawing.

Listen and colour and draw in the picture on page 4.

 # Never, sometimes, often, usually, always

Read this part of the story. Find *sometimes, often* and *usually.*

> I didn't often see my uncle when I was a child because he lived in Africa, but he came to see us sometimes. When he did, he usually told me one of his stories.

What does Ben say to his brother?

Choose the best answer. Write a letter (A–H).

Example: Where's my dinner?

 ...B....

1 Why didn't you make any soup?

....

2 You can't read!

....

3 What are you reading about?

....

4 And where did you find that

silver cup?

....

5 Give that cup to me!

....

A Yes, I can.

B I haven't made it.

C OK, but hold it carefully.

D Can you eat it?

E No, they're in that box.

F Different parts of the world.

G Because I wanted to read.

H It was in the field.

Ben's lucky day!

Complete the sentences. Write 1, 2, 3 or 4 words.

Example: Ben found the ....old silver cup.... on the ground.

1 Ben used his .... to clean the cup.

2 There was only .... in Ben's bag.

3 Ben wanted .... because he felt cold and thirsty.

4 Ben was very .... when he saw the hot chocolate.

5 Ben felt cold because his .... had lots of holes in it.

6 Ben's beautiful new coat felt ....

 Differences

Talk about Ben. Talk about a friend.

Ben		**My friend's name** ....
Brothers/sisters?	two brothers	Brothers/sisters? ....
Where/live?	on a farm	Where/live? ....
Age?	ten	Age? ....
What/want?	new coat	What/want? ....
What/like doing?	reading	What/like doing? ....

anywhereeverywheresomewherenowhere

Complete the sentences with words from the above line.

1 Ben found the silver cup .... in the fields.

2 There were books .... ! They were on the table, next to his bed and by the fire.

3 After the cup broke, Ben's brothers looked for the money, but it was .... in the house.

4 Ben's coat wasn't by the door or on his chair. Ben couldn't find it ....

(J) What did Ben do next?

Look at the pictures and sentences. Tell the story.

Ben started going ....
He liked learning about
....

Ben's .... gave him a
lot of .... He usually
studied hard in ....

Ben left school when he was
.... He wanted to visit
a lot of ....

Ben went to ....
He learnt everything about
....

(K) Ben learnt about gorillas.

Choose the right word. Write it on the line.

There are three kinds of gorillas, but Ben went to Africa to learn ...*about*... Mountain Gorillas.	after into	about
These live in the jungle and in forests. They only		
1 live .... People often think that gorillas	there then	where
2 are dangerous animals but they only	get gets	getting
angry and fight if their group is in danger. Father		
3 gorillas are called Silverbacks because	how when	why
they get older, the hair on their backs goes silver.		
Mountain Gorillas eat fruit, leaves and flowers.		
4 They very .... eat small insects too. They	often always	never
spend all day eating, playing and looking after		
the younger gorillas. There are only about 700		
5 Mountain Gorillas .... the world. It is	in on	at
6 important that we all find out about .... !	they theirs	them

(L) Play the game. Find the jungle animals!

11

Emma was on holiday with her parents and she was bored. There were too many people in the swimming pool. She had no-one to play tennis with and her mum and dad just wanted to sit in the sun, so Emma walked down to the beach and sat on the sand.

'What a boring day!' she thought.

Then something hit her on the head. It was a beach ball.

'Sorry!' a little boy said. He picked up his ball and stood in front of her. He was only about six or seven. Emma wanted him to go away.

'What do you want?' Emma asked him.

'Nothing,' he said. 'But you look unhappy. What's the matter?'

'I'm bored,' Emma said.

'We could look for treasure,' the little boy said.

Emma thought that was a silly idea. 'Where are your parents?' she asked.

'They're on our ship, out there by the island. I'm the son of a pirate,' he said.

Emma laughed. 'There's no ship and you can't be a pirate,' she said. 'Pirates are only in stories.'

The boy didn't move. 'I *am* the son of a pirate and our ship *is* there. You can't see it because you believe that we're only in stories.'

Emma thought the little boy was funny, and suddenly she didn't feel bored. 'OK,' she said, and stood up. 'Let's look for treasure!'

The boy pointed at some rocks. 'Shall we look there?' he whispered.

Between the rocks there were lots of pools of sea water. They were full of small fish and shells.

'Those shells are lovely, aren't they?' the little boy said. 'They're a kind of treasure.'

'Hmmm,' Emma said. Then she saw something blue in the rock pool too.

'What's that? It's a glove, isn't it?'

'Yes,' the little boy said. 'Perhaps someone lost it here in the winter.' He picked up the wet glove. 'This is a kind of treasure too,' he said, and put it in a big bag that he carried on his shoulder.

Look! What's that?

There was something at the bottom of the next rock pool too.

'What's that?' Emma asked. 'It looks like a silver fork. Can you get it for me?'

'Of course,' said the little boy. He pulled out the silver fork and put it in his bag too.

Then Emma saw something else. There was an old pair of glasses in another rock pool. She pointed to them and the little boy pulled them out.

'More treasure!' he laughed.

Then they arrived at another rock pool. Emma and the little boy looked down into the water. It was very, very deep.

'It's dangerous here,' Emma said. 'Come on. Let's go back to the beach.'

But the little boy said, 'Look! There's a ring under that black and gold fish. I'll get it for you. That's the best kind of treasure!'

'But the water's too deep. That fish has got very big teeth. It looks angry. And that crab might bite you too!' Emma said.

The little boy put his bag down on the rock. 'I'm not afraid. I'm the son of a pirate, so deep water, fish with big teeth and crabs aren't problems for me,' he said.

The little boy took out the glove, the fork and the old pair of glasses. He put the glove on his hand. Then he put the old pair of glasses on to the end of the fork and put his hand and arm into the deep water. The fish couldn't bite through the glove and the little boy hooked the ring out of the water with the end of the glasses. He gave it to Emma.

The ring was beautiful, but when Emma looked up to say thank you to the little boy, he wasn't there. She was very surprised.

Where was he? Emma didn't know, but she carried the ring carefully back to the hotel to show her parents. They weren't sitting in the sun, so Emma went upstairs to their room. Emma's mother was there. She looked very sad.

'What's the matter, Mum?' Emma asked.

'I've lost my beautiful gold ring. I went for a swim in the sea and it came off my finger.'

Emma opened her hand. 'Is this it?' she asked.

'Yes!' her mother said. 'Where did you find it?'

'The son of a pirate found it in a rock pool,' Emma answered.

Emma looked out of the hotel window. A pirate ship was sailing away and a little boy was waving to her.

And this time, Emma could see them both – the son of a pirate *and* the pirate ship!

The glove, the fork and the old pair of glasses

2

A New words for you!

Draw lines between the green words and different parts of the picture.

This black fish only lives in water that's very deep.

This angry red fish likes biting fingers!

This young boy is trying to hook the green fish.

B What happened next?

Write 2–6 in the stars. Draw lines to show the right order.

1. Emma and the little boy walked to the rocks.

The son of a pirate found a ring.

Emma felt bored.

Emma could see the pirate ship.

Emma's mum felt very sad.

Emma saw a glove in the water.

C Who said this?

Write A, B or C.   A Emma   B the little boy   C Emma's mum

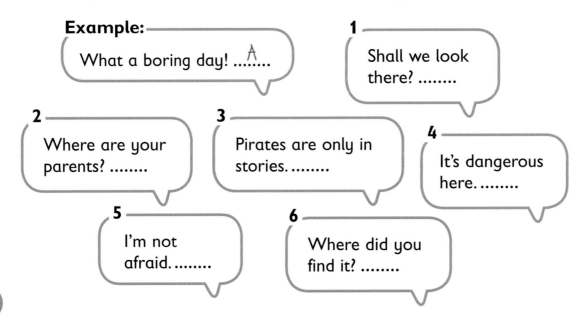

Example:
What a boring day! ...A....

1
Shall we look there? ....

2
Where are your parents? ....

3
Pirates are only in stories. ....

4
It's dangerous here. ....

5
I'm not afraid. ....

6
Where did you find it? ....

D Who? Which? Where? What? How old?

Answer the questions. Write 1, 2 or 3 words.

Example: Who went with Emma on her holiday? ....her parents...........

1 Which sport did Emma want to play? ....

2 Where did Emma walk to? ....

3 What did Emma sit on? ....

4 What hit Emma on her head? ....

5 How old was the little boy? ....

6 What did the little boy ask Emma? '...........................'

E Isn't it? Aren't they?

Complete the questions. Write _isn't it?_ or _aren't they?_

Examples: It's a glove, ...isn't it?...........

Those shells are lovely, ...aren't they?...........

1 Those glasses are old, ...

2 The water is deep, ...

3 It's Emma's mum's ring, ...

4 The pirates are on their ship now, ...

F Sand, sea, sky and a shark!

Look at the picture and tell the story.

1 ....

2 ....

3 ....

G CD1 05 Let's draw!

Listen and draw 5 things in the picture on page 14.

What's this? What are these?

Write the answer on the line.

Example: You can use this to get dry after a swim.   ...a towel...

1   You can pick food up with this.   ....

2   These wave in the wind on the tops of boats.   ....

3   On cold days, you can wear these on your hands.   ....

4   This insect has beautiful wings.   ....

5   This fish is dangerous because it has big teeth!   ....

 Change part of the story.

Cross out the green words and choose new words.

Emma was on holiday with her ~~parents~~ ...best friend... and she was

bored. There were too many people in the swimming pool

(1) .... She had no-one to play tennis **(2)** ....

with and her mum and dad **(3)** .... just wanted to sit in

the sun **(4)** .... , so Emma walked down to the beach

(5) .... and sat on the sand **(6)** ....

 ○CD1 06 **What will Emma do?**

**Listen to Emma, Emma's dad and Emma's mum.
Tick the box.**

Example:

Words that sound the same

Find words in the story that sound like these other words.

Example: It sounds like chips but you can cross ....ships..........

the sea in these!

1 It sounds like day but you do this with games. ....

2 It sounds like sad but this is your father. ....

3 It sounds like fun but you see this in the sky. ....

4 It sounds like hand but you find this on the beach. ....

5 It sounds like fall but you can catch and throw this. ....

6 It sounds like bed but this is the top part of your body. ....

 CD1 07 The pirate's poem!

Can you guess the missing words? Listen and write.

I like swimming

   in the salty sea

and .... for crabs

   to .... to me!

I like skipping

   on sailing ships

and .... big fish

   to .... with chips!

Talk about things you like doing.

 Play the game. I'm feeling happy!

Robert and the three envelopes

Robert lived in a flat in a tall grey building in the middle of a big city. When he looked out of his window, he could only see more tall grey buildings and lots of roads and noisy traffic. Sometimes, this made Robert feel sad. He liked watching television programmes about climbing mountains and going to places where there were waterfalls, lakes and beautiful beaches. He loved reading stories about ships that sailed across the sea and about people who lived on strange islands or in other exciting places.

'Why must we live here in the city?' he asked his mother.

'Because my job at the busy hospital is here, Robert. But perhaps we can have a nice holiday in the countryside next summer. Would you like that?'

'Oh yes!' Robert laughed.

That night, when Robert went to bed he thought about going on holiday. But then he remembered something. Last year, his mother said the same thing, but they didn't go to the countryside. They spent the summer at home in the city because they didn't have enough money to buy train tickets or stay in a hotel in the countryside.

On the school bus the next morning, Robert looked through the window and saw a boat on the river in the middle of the city.

'I'd like to go on a boat or on a big ship one day,' he thought. Then he saw a train on a bridge near the city station. 'I'd like to go on a fast train one day,' he thought. Then he looked up into the sky and saw a plane. 'I'd like to go on a plane one day too. I'd like to look out of its windows at the countryside below,' he thought.

When school finished, Robert didn't want to go home by bus. He decided to walk. He walked past the shoe factory, the chemist's and then past the police station at the bottom of the hill. Then he walked past the supermarket and the bread shop. But then he started to feel tired, so he sat down for a minute on a wall outside the post office.

Then a strange thing happened. A big black and white bird flew down from the sky. It had an envelope in its beak. It dropped the envelope on Robert's foot and then flew away again. Robert picked the letter up. On the envelope, it said 'Read me'. So Robert did!

Robert opened the envelope. There was a piece of blue paper inside with some writing on it. Robert read it carefully.

'If you find me, go and look in your biggest, oldest book.'

Robert couldn't understand the message but he put the piece of paper in his pocket.

When he got home he sat down and looked at the message again.

' "In your biggest, oldest book",' he thought. 'What does that mean?'

Robert decided to try something. He got a chair from the kitchen and carried it into the living room. Then he put the chair in

In my biggest, oldest book?

front of the bookcase and stood on it. The biggest and oldest book was at the top of the bookcase. Robert took it down from the shelf. It was very heavy.

Robert opened it and a thin envelope fell out. Inside the envelope was a little book. Its pages were yellow because they were so old, and they had lots of numbers on them. He jumped down and ran back into the kitchen to show the little book to his mother.

'What's this?' he asked her. His mother took the book and opened it.

'It's the kind of book that banks gave people a long time ago,' she said. 'This person had lots of money in the bank. And look! There's a name on the front. It says "Helen Bird". I don't believe it! That was my grandmother's name! I'll go to the bank tomorrow and show this to Mr Flag.'

When Robert's mother gave the old book to Mr Flag the next day, he looked at it very carefully, picked up his telephone and spoke to someone in an excited kind of way. Then he put the telephone down again. He had a big smile on his face.

'Well,' he said, 'you must thank your son for finding this little book. Your grandmother left all this money in our bank for you a long time ago, but we didn't know that until now. What are you going to buy with it?'

Robert's mother smiled. 'Something that Robert wants very much.'

When Robert came home from school later that afternoon, he found a bigger envelope on the kitchen table. 'Open it!' his mother said.

Inside the envelope were two plane tickets and two train tickets and two boat tickets!

'Robert, Mr Flag at the bank says we've got enough money now. We're going to have a wonderful holiday.'

'Because of your grandmother's little book?' Robert asked.

'Yes,' his mother said.

Robert looked out of the window at the sky. He couldn't see the big black and white bird high in the clouds, but he knew the bird was there.

Thank you!

'And because of the big black and white bird!' Robert smiled.

'What do you mean?' his mother asked.

'That's my secret!' Robert said.

Robert and the three envelopes

 New words for you!

Draw lines between your new words and the pictures.

building

beak

ship

message

middle

B Can you remember?

Answer the questions. Use 1, 2 or 3 words.

Example: Where does Robert live? .... in a flat ....

1 Did Robert go on holiday last year? ....

2 What dropped a letter on Robert's foot? ....

3 Did Robert find the old book at home or
   in the street? ....

4 Was Robert's mother happy, angry or sad
   about the book? ....

5 Can Robert and his mother go on a holiday
   now? ....

 What happened next?

Put the pictures in the right order. Write 2–5 in the boxes.

A   B   C   D   E

☐   ☐   1   ☐   ☐

D Robert's home in the city

Complete the sentences. Write 2 words.

Example: Robert's flat was in the middle of a ....big.city.......... .

1 Robert could see lots of .... from his window.

2 Robert enjoyed reading about ships and people who lived in
.... !

3 Robert's mother worked at a .... in the city.

4 Robert wanted to have a .... in the countryside
next summer.

5 Robert and his mother couldn't stay in a hotel last year because they
didn't have ....

E Opposites!

Find words on page 20 that have opposite meanings to these.

Example: small ....big.........

1 boring ....   2 ugly ....   3 quiet ....

4 happy ....   5 horrible ....

F (CD1 09) Do some drawing.

Listen and draw in the picture on page 20.

G I'd like to ...

Read this part of the story.

'I'd like to go on a boat or on a big ship one
day,' he thought. Then he saw a train on a
bridge near the city station. 'I'd like to go on
a fast train one day,' he thought. Then he
looked up into the sky and saw a plane. 'I'd
like to go on a plane one day too.'

Which 3 things would *you* like to do one day?

H Find the differences.

Look at the picture on page 21 and at this picture. Find 6 differences.

I Another story!

Choose a word for each space.

Katy sat down for a minute on a ....*chair*........ outside the
(1) .... Then a strange thing happened. A small brown
and white **(2)** .... ran down the hill. It had a box in its
(3) .... It **(4)** .... the box on Katy's foot and
then ran away again. Katy picked the box up. On the box, it said
'**(5)** .... me'. So Katy did!

J ○CD1 10 Where shall I put all these letters?

Listen and draw lines.

K Robert's rucksack

Choose 8 things for Robert.

- ....
- ....
- ....
- ....

L Robert's holiday postcard!

Choose the right word. Write it on the line.

Hi!

We're having a ...great... time! The food
1 here is much .... than we have at
home! We 're staying in a hotel next to
2 the .... waterfall in the world. The
3 water's very .... ! We went to the
4 bottom of the waterfall in a .... boat
yesterday. Everyone laughed because we
5 got so .... I think the people here
6 are .... than in London. The
7 weather's .... than at home too!

....

I'd like to live here! See you soon! Robert

great	greater	greatest
nice	nicer	nicest
high	higher	highest
loud	louder	loudest
small	smaller	smallest
wet	wetter	wettest
friendly	friendlier	friendliest
sunny	sunnier	sunniest

M Play the game. Holiday shopping!

What do you want to buy on holiday?

Lara is my mother's best friend. She's a vet, that's a doctor who looks after sick animals. I want to be a vet too. One day I asked her, 'Why did you decide to be a vet, Lara?'

'It's a strange story,' she answered. 'When I was your age, I had no brothers or sisters to play with, so in the winter holidays I stayed with my three cousins who lived high up in the mountains. They were tall and strong and could ski very fast. They were very good at climbing too. But I couldn't ski or climb. My legs weren't strong enough! I was often ill too, so I had to carry different medicines with me all the time.

'One day, my cousins wanted to climb the mountain that was behind their house. They said, "You must come with us, Lara!" They were unkind. They knew I wasn't well enough or brave enough.

'I walked a little way, but I was soon tired, so I had to stop and sit down. My cousins laughed at my red face. "See you later, then!" they called and went on up the mountain without me.

'I started to feel better after a few minutes, but then I heard an animal behind me. I felt a big, warm, furry, soft face on my shoulder. It was a mountain lion.'

'Wow!' I said.

'I was very afraid,' Lara said, 'but I couldn't run away because my legs still felt weak, so I just sat there. The lion opened its mouth—'

'Oh no!' I said.

'—and said, "I've got a terrible toothache." Well, I knew all about toothache because I often had that, so I gave it some medicine that was in my jacket pocket,' Lara said.

I laughed and said, 'I don't believe you, Lara!'

'Why not?' she asked. 'Strange things happen in the world all the time!'

'The lion and I sat and talked about cakes and snakes and other things and after a few minutes, it said, "My tooth's feeling much better now, but I've got a very bad stomach-ache. I ate too much food after I woke up this morning."

'I often had stomach-ache, so I had a bottle of stomach-ache medicine in my rucksack. I put some on a little plastic spoon and gave it to the lion and then we sat and talked about parks and sharks and other things.

'After a few minutes, the lion said, "My stomach's feeling much better now, but I've got a horrible headache. I lay in the sun for hours yesterday."

'I knew about headaches, so I took a clean handkerchief from my jacket pocket and put it in the snow before I put it on the lion's furry head. "That's very cold but it feels good!" the lion said.

'Then we sat and talked about tails and whales and other things. But suddenly, the lion jumped up and said, "I'm feeling grrrrreat now! What shall we do next?"

'I pointed at the mountain. My cousins were already high up above us. "Can you take me up to the top?" I asked.

'"Sure!" it said. "You can ride on my back. No problem!" So I jumped on its back and put both arms round its neck.

'The lion ran faster than the wind. It's really wonderful to ride on a lion's back. Have you ever done that?' Lara asked me.

'No!' I said and laughed.

'Well, you must try it one day. But we have to finish the story ...

'When the mountain lion and I arrived at the top, I got off its back, and it disappeared into a dark cave. Soon after that, my cousins arrived. They were very surprised when they saw me.'

'What happened next?' I asked.

'Well,' said Lara, 'they never laughed at me again! And every year, I went back to the place where I met the lion and it came to talk to me again. Sometimes I took it more medicine and I often rode on its back in the snow. We became great friends and I knew that I wanted to be a vet one day. So that's the answer to your question.'

Lara waited for a minute and then laughed.

'I'm sorry,' she said. 'It's just a story.'

But then she turned round and looked at a photo on her desk. It was of a little girl and a mountain lion. They were sitting on a rock in the snow and the lion had its big, soft, furry face on her shoulder.

Lara turned back and smiled at me. 'Now I must work,' she said. 'Would you like some more orange juice before you go?'

Lara and the mountain lion

A New words for you!

Draw lines between your new words and their meanings.

unkind   ill

   furry   lovely

sick   has lots of fur

   wonderful   not kind

B Who or what said this?

Write A, B or C.

A   B   C

Example:

Why did you decide to be a vet? C

1 I couldn't ski or climb. .....

2 I've got a terrible toothache. .....

3 I ate too much food. .....

4 Can you take me up to the top? .....

5 What happened next? .....

6 It's just a story. .....

C What happened next?

Put the sentences in the right order. Write 2–8 in the boxes.

Lara rode on the lion's back. ☐   Lara went to see her cousins. ☐

A lion came and talked to Lara. ☐   The boy visited Lara's office. 1

Lara felt tired on the mountain. ☐   Lara decided to be a vet. 9

Lara started to tell the boy a story. ☐

The lion had some of Lara's medicine. ☐

Lara and her cousins began to climb a mountain. ☐

D Lara's office

Look at the picture. Write *yes* or *no*.

Example:

There's a balcony outside the door of Lara's office.

.yes......

1	One of the photos on the wall has a monkey in it.	....
2	Lara has ridden a camel in a hot country.	....
3	Lara's kitten has a tail which is grey and white.	....
4	The boy is holding a drink in his left hand.	....
5	Lara is writing something on one of the pieces of paper.	....
6	You can see grey squares on the floor of the office.	....

E So

Draw lines to join the two halves of each sentence.

Example:

Lara had no brothers or sisters, **so** she often had to take medicine.

1 Lara's cousins lived in the mountains, **so** she had to stop and sit down.

2 Lara had weak legs, **so** her cousins went on without her.

3 Lara was often ill, **so** she wasn't good at climbing or skiing.

4 Lara got tired quickly on the walk, **so** she stayed with her cousins in the holidays.

5 Lara couldn't go on up the mountain, **so** they were very good at skiing.

F Lara's medicine

Complete the sentences. Write 1, 2 or 3 words.

Example: The toothache medicine was in

Lara's ....*jacket pocket*.... .

1   The lion's tooth felt .... after a few minutes.
2   The lion's .... hurt because it had too much food.
3   Lara put the lion's stomach-ache medicine on a ....
4   The lion sat in the sun for hours, so it had a horrible ....
5   Lara put a handkerchief that was .... on the lion's head.

G Was it before or after this?

Cross out the wrong word in each sentence. Write one more sentence.

Example: The lion felt ill before/~~after~~ it saw Lara.

1   The lion came to Lara before/after her cousins went on without her.
2   Lara felt tired before/after she sat down.
3   The lion felt much better before/after Lara gave it some medicine.
4   The lion had a headache before/after it sat in the sun.
5   .... before/after ....

H What's the matter, Lara?

What do Lara and the lion say? Match the sentences.

I can't pick my rucksack up because my shoulder hurts. ◯   My feet are cold! ◯   I'm hungry! ◯

I cut my hand when I jumped off that rock. ◯

A   Oh no! I'll help you clean it.

B   No problem! I can get it for you.

C   Me too! I'll find some fruit.

Can you help me? I'm too tired to walk. ◯

D   Sure! You can ride on my back!

E   Oh dear! Sit nearer the fire.

I CD1 12 After Lara met the mountain lion, she ...

Listen and write a letter in each box.

Monday   `C`
Tuesday   ☐
Wednesday   ☐
Thursday   ☐
Friday   ☐
Saturday   ☐

J CD1 13 Who's afraid? Not me!

Listen and write.

1 There's a lion on that mountain
and another in this cave,
but I just .... and call to it,
'Can you see me? I'm so .... !'

2 There's a monster right .... me
I can smell it in the .... ,
but I just turn and say to it,
'You need to comb your hair.'

3 I climb the highest rock
and I see a hungry snake,
but I just wave and .... it,
'Would you like a piece of .... ?'

4 There's a lion in my ....
It's a friendly one I .... ,
but if one asks to be *YOUR* friend,
smile kindly and say, '*NO!*'

K What do you want to be one day?

A vet? A singer? A doctor? An engineer? An astronaut? A policeman
or policewoman? A taxi driver? A tennis player? A dentist?
A businesswoman or businessman? A journalist?

Big Nose and the Storm-Maker

No-one knew Big Nose's real name but everyone knew that he had the biggest nose in the village. His nose was enormous and everyone laughed and pointed at it. 'Look at that big nose!' they called.

This made Big Nose unhappy, so he only went into the village when he needed to buy chocolate or a new handkerchief.

The part of the country where Big Nose and the villagers lived was by the sea. There were no hills there, just fields where the farmers grew vegetables to sell in the city. Children played games outside in the streets and when the weather was warm and sunny, they ran down to the beach to look for shells or to play in the water.

Big Nose liked being on the beach too. He loved the smell of the sea and because his nose was so big, he could smell very well. He could smell the dinner that people were eating on islands that were far away and all the different fish that lived in the sea too. He liked the smell of octopuses most of all and often caught them and cooked them for his breakfast.

Big Nose could smell the difference between the north, the south, the east and the west winds too. His nose could (perhaps) smell better than any other nose in the world.

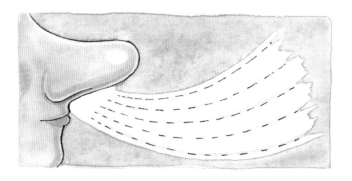

One evening, Big Nose was walking on the sand, enjoying the smell of the salt in the sea and the warm south wind, when suddenly the wind changed and started blowing from the north. Big Nose shivered. He looked at the sky and smelled the air. 'Oh no!' he thought. 'I know that smell and I know that sound in the wind too. It smells like and it sounds like the Storm-Maker.'

'Storm-Maker,' he called out loudly, 'I can't see you yet, but you can't hide from me. You should go away!'

The Storm-Maker said nothing.

'Storm-Maker!' Big Nose called more loudly into the north wind. 'You may wish to visit our village today but we don't want your heavy rain, your loud thunder or your dangerous lightning here. Go away! Take your problems to another part of the world.'

But the Storm-Maker didn't listen. It began to mix up the winds with its enormous spoon to make big black clouds, and the rain came down like waterfalls. The waves in the sea got bigger and bigger and Big Nose suddenly saw lightning that looked like a big silver knife cutting through the dark grey sky. Then he heard thunder that sounded like the angriest, most frightening drum in the world.

Big Nose got angry too. He stood up slowly and looked at the face of the Storm-Maker and began to whistle at it. But the Storm-Maker still didn't go away. The sand blew and blew, the wind got stronger and stronger and the rain got heavier and heavier.

Back in the village, hats and leaves and umbrellas were flying away in the wind. Children were hiding under tables and parents were brushing the rain water away from their doors and worrying about the vegetables in their fields.

Big Nose climbed to the top of the highest rock on the beach and looked straight into the eye of the Storm-Maker. He took more and more air in through his enormous nose and whistled more and more loudly until his whistling was louder than the wind.

In the end, the Storm-Maker put its enormous hands over its enormous ears and slowly, slowly, turned away from the sky over the village. Its black clouds disappeared and the wind was quiet again.

'That's better!' Big Nose said quietly and climbed down from the high rock and walked slowly home.

And from behind the rock, two small children who were too afraid to move or shout for help in the storm, got up, picked up their bags of shells and ran back to the village.

When they got home, they told the oldest woman in the village about Big Nose. She told the story to her sons and daughters. They told it to their husbands, wives, sons, daughters, grandsons and granddaughters, and then everyone told the story to ten more people! Soon everyone in the village knew about Big Nose and the Storm-Maker.

Good morning!

How are you this morning?

When Big Nose walked into the village the next day, no-one laughed or pointed at his big nose or said that his whistling gave them earache (which was true). They knew that Big Nose made the Storm-Maker take away its terrible rain, loud thunder and dangerous lightning, so they smiled at him and said, 'Good morning!' or 'How are you?' One small child gave him a beautiful flower.

Big Nose was surprised. Everyone was being so nice to him! But he didn't want to ask why. He just said, 'I'm fine, thank you!' and smiled back at everyone and felt much, much, much happier!

Big Nose and the Storm-Maker

A New words for you!

Draw lines between your new words and the pictures.

thunder

lightning

disappear

shiver

blow

B Can you remember?

Cross out the 2 wrong words in each sentence.

Example: Big Nose lived near a beach/~~mountain~~/~~city~~.

1   The people in the village laughed/shouted/waved at Big Nose.

2   They grew flowers/vegetables/fruit in their fields.

3   Big Nose liked eating octopuses/oranges/onions.

4   He was very good at whispering/walking/whistling.

5   Big Nose made the fire/village/storm go away.

6   At the end of the story, Big Nose was hungrier/happier/heavier.

C Who's talking about this story?

Tick the right box.

☐ David

The middle of the story made me angry. I thought the man was horrible when he shouted at the other people.

☐ Sarah

The end of the story made me happy again. The people who were unkind to the man before, were nicer to him.

☐ Jane

This story made me hungry because I love eating fish too! I liked the part when the man caught the octopus!

D CD1 15 **Who's in the village?**

Write these names round the first picture in the story.

Harry   Betty   Daisy   Tony   Lucy   Katy

Listen and draw lines from the names to the people in the picture.

 E **What's the weather like today?**

Look at the pictures and complete the sentences.

Example: Take an umbrella! Look at the ....rain......... outside!

1   I'm feeling afraid. I hate the sound of .... !

2   It's so .... today. I can't see anything outside.

3   Look at that big black .... in the sky!

4   I love .... weather. I like feeling warm.

5   A .... is coming. Look! Lightning!

6   It's sunny and it's .... today. Great! Let's go sailing!

F **What does the Storm-Maker say to Big Nose?**

Choose the best answer. Write a letter (A–H).

1   I can't see you yet, but I can smell you.

     ....

2   Where did you come from?

     ....

3   What are you doing now?

     ....

4   Your lightning is frightening.

     ....

5   You should go away.

     ....

A Can it?

B I don't want to. Sorry!

C The north of the country.

D So do I.

E Can you?

F No, it's an enormous spoon.

G I know it is!

H I'm making my thunder!

The Storm-Maker's coming!

Complete the sentences. Write 1 or 2 words.

Example: Big Nose didn't want the Storm-Maker to

visit ....*the village*.... .

1 But the .... didn't want to listen to Big Nose.

2 It used an .... to mix up the winds.

3 Then Big Nose saw .... that were big and black.

4 The .... cut through the grey sky like a knife.

5 And the .... sounded like a very angry drum.

6 Big Nose began to feel very .... too.

7 But the wind just got stronger and the .... got heavier.

 CD1 16 **That sounds like ...**

Listen, whisper to your partner, then write the word.

1 We think that's the ....

2 That's the ....

3 That sounds like a ....　　**4** And that's the ....

5 We know! Those are ....　　**6** That sounds like .... !

 It looks like ...

What does Big Nose think the 4 things in picture A look like?
What does Big Nose think the 4 things in picture B smell like?

J A different ending?

Choose 10 words from the cloud to put in the spaces.

The next day, Big Nose walked into the village but he couldn't ......see...... anyone in the street. It was very quiet! But then he walked round a **(1)** .... and all the people came out of their houses with big **(2)** .... on their faces. The children were laughing and **(3)** .... up and down. Big Nose was very **(4)** .... ! 'We're going to have a **(5)** .... and it's for you!' a small girl said. 'Thank you so much for making the **(6)** .... Storm-Maker go away!' an old woman said. 'Thank you for **(7)** .... the storm!' one of the farmers added. 'We're sorry we **(8)** .... at you!' two young brothers said. Big Nose smiled back at everyone and felt much, much, much happier!

party
laughed
surprised
~~see~~
corner
stopping
air
jumping
horrible
smiles

K CD1 17 The weather news!

Listen and draw the right weather in each part of the country.

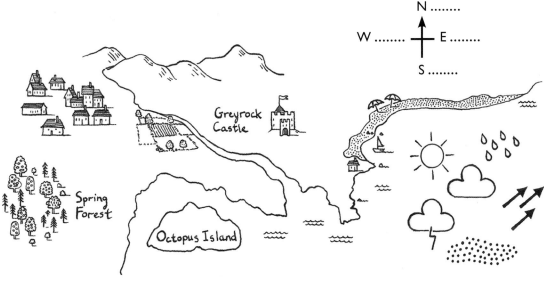

N ....
W .... E ....
S ....

L Play the game. What shall we do next?

Look at the weather cards and talk to your friends.

6 Michael and the red rug

Michael was happy. He liked having fun with his friends, playing computer games, riding bikes and watching soccer on TV. He liked his school, his teachers and all his classmates too. He was in the school volleyball team. He loved his room, his home and the street where he and his parents lived. Everything was fine until one Monday evening. Michael was watching TV when the phone rang. His father answered it. At the end of the phone call, Michael's dad said, 'I've got a new job!'

But the new job was in the north of the country in a place that was 300 kilometres away.

His father was excited and his mother was surprised and very happy, but every time Michael thought about leaving his friends and school and the town where they lived, he felt unhappy and angry. 'I want to stay here,' he thought. 'I don't want to go and live somewhere different.'

Michael's parents tried to make him feel better. They said the new town was great and that he could make lots of new friends there, but Michael didn't want to talk about it. They showed him photos of their lovely new home on the internet, but Michael didn't want to look at them, so he didn't!

Soon it was March 13th – the day when the family had to move. The family got in their yellow truck and drove north to their new home. Michael listened to music all the way there. He didn't want to speak to anyone.

When they arrived, Michael's dad gave him a key. 'Open the front door, Michael,' he said. 'Go upstairs and choose your room. We're going to look at the garden at the back of the house.'

Michael opened the door and went inside. There was nothing in any of the rooms. The house felt cold and empty. He went upstairs and looked in the first room. He didn't like it – it smelled strange. He looked in the second room – that one was too dark. But the third room seemed friendlier. There was an old red rug on the floor. Michael sat on it. 'I'll have this room,' he decided. He looked at his watch. It said a quarter past three. 'Hmm,' he thought. 'The truck with all our things in it will arrive soon.'

Then something very strange began to happen.

The rug started to turn round and round and round and, because he was on it, Michael turned round and round and round with it!

Something very strange was happening to his watch too. The numbers on it were changing very fast. It was one minute to midnight, then suddenly it was midday, then half past four, then a quarter to eight. The dates on his watch were changing quickly too!

When the rug stopped turning, Michael looked at his watch again. It was a quarter past three on April 21st! Michael couldn't understand. It was more than a month later!

Michael felt dizzy for a minute but then he stood up and looked round the room. He couldn't believe his eyes. The room wasn't empty now. It was full! There was a new bed behind him and some big blue cushions in the corner by the door. His rucksack, with lots of interesting school books in it, was on a desk. He could hear some children outside. They were laughing. Then his phone began to ring. Michael took it out of his pocket and answered it.

'Hi, Michael,' someone said. 'You're late! Come on! The volleyball game will start in 20 minutes and we need you! You're our best player. Oh! And Tony's going to have a pool party this evening. It's his birthday. Can you come?'

'Ermm, yes, sure,' Michael began to say. Then suddenly everything started turning round and round again. 'Am I going to go even more into the future?' he thought.

But when the rug stopped turning, the room was empty again.
The date on his watch was March 13th again too. Michael could
hear his parents. They were inside the house now. He could hear
them on the stairs.

His dad opened the door.

'Hi! What a great room!' he said.
'How are you doing?'

'I'm feeling happier,' Michael said. 'I'm
feeling much, much happier. I think I'm
going to make lots of good friends here.'

'That's great,' his dad answered, 'but bring
that old red rug downstairs. The truck
with all our things in it has just arrived. The driver can take it away
with him.'

Michael smiled. 'I like it, Dad,' he said.

'Well, OK. It can stay here, if you want. But I think we'll buy you a
new bed and you can choose some posters to put on these walls,' his
dad answered.

'And how about some big blue cushions for me to sit on in that
corner? And can I have a new volleyball too?' Michael asked.

'Sure!' Michael's dad said. 'That sounds like a great idea!'

Michael and the red rug

6

A New words for you!

Choose a word to complete each sentence.

I've got a red .... in the middle of my room.

Listen! Your phone's ....

I got .... when I turned round.

I like sitting on big ....

rug
cushions
ringing
dizzy

B What happened next?

Put the pictures in the right order. Write 2–6 in the boxes.

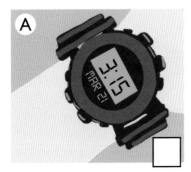

A

B

C

D

1

E

F

C Can you remember?

Cross out the 2 wrong words in each sentence.

Example: Michael was good at playing volleyball/soccer/tennis.

1 Michael's dad got a new bike/job/pet.
2 Michael chose the first/second/third room.
3 The time on Michael's watch/computer/clock changed.
4 Michael's father/brother/mother came into his new room.
5 The cushions in Michael's new room will be green/blue/yellow.

Michael didn't want to move.

Complete the sentences. Write 2 or 3 words.

Example: Michael enjoyed playing ...computer games... with his friends.

1 .... got a phone call about a job.

2 The new job was .... away from Michael's home town.

3 Michael felt .... about leaving his friends.

4 Michael didn't want to look at the pictures of their .... on the internet.

5 Michael's family drove north in their ....

 Opposites!

Find words on page 44 that have opposite meanings to these.

Example: south ...north...

1 bored .... 2 happy .... 3 same ....

4 worse .... 5 horrible ....

  Do some colouring.

Listen and colour the second picture on page 45.

G **Telling the time**

Read this part of the story.
Then talk about times.

It was one minute to midnight, then suddenly it was midday, then half past four, then a quarter to eight. The dates on his watch were changing quickly too! When the rug stopped turning, Michael looked at his watch again. It was a quarter past three on April 21st.

What's the time now? What time will school finish today?

What time did you get up this morning? What time will you go to bed?

H **What was happening when the rug stopped turning?**

Find the right ending. Draw lines.

When the rug stopped turning the first time …

1 some children — were singing in the trees.

2 the birds — was flying round the room.

3 two men in a truck — were driving up the street.

4 a boy on a bike — were laughing outside.

5 a butterfly — was riding past the house.

 I **Dizzy and busy**

Find the matching sound.

dizzy   stood   eyes   full   new   bed   some   laugh   hi!   late

you   half   busy   mum   my

cries   said   wool   would

eight

 J **Change part of the story.**

Look at the words in the box. Choose a word for each space.

Michael felt ...*afraid*... for a minute but then he stood up

and **(1)** .... round the room. He couldn't believe his

eyes. The room wasn't empty now. It was full! There was a

new **(2)** .... behind him and some big blue

(3) .... in the corner by the door. His rucksack,

with lots of **(4)** .... school books in it, was on

a desk. He could **(5)** .... some children outside.

They were **(6)** .... Then his phone began to

ring. Michael took it out of his pocket and answered it.

> ~~afraid~~   see   torch   boxes   walked   raining   forget
> dropped   shouting   problems   heavy   team

Please come to my pool party!

Complete Tony's message.

Hi Michael!

It's my birthday. I'm going to have a pool party! Can you come? You'll make lots of new friends there. Tony

Date: ....

Time: ....

Address: ....

Please bring: ....

Wear: ....

 My new home

Choose your new home and talk about it!

My new home		.... 's new home	
Address: ...... Green Street		Address: ...... Green Street	
Next to?	....	....	
House/warm/cold?	....	....	
Colour/walls?	....	....	
Nicest room?	....	....	

 For my new room, I'd like ...

Choose things for your new room.

Ruby's 11 and she loves making things. She's loved making all kinds of things since she was about three. Her parents didn't buy her dolls or clothes for birthday presents. They gave her paint, glue, scissors and pieces of wood!

Ruby wants to be an engineer. She made a brilliant toy racing car six months ago. 'And I'm going to make the fastest racing car in the world one day,' she told her grandfather.

Last month, Ruby was walking past the town fire station when she saw a poster on the wall. It said:

**Under 12s
Bike Race**

21 kilometres

Sunday June 18th

**Email
Richard.Black@met.au**

**or phone 933572
to find out more**

Ruby knew her bicycle wasn't fast enough to win a race. It was also too small for her now. 'Perhaps I can make a new one!' she thought.

'Could I have the old metal lamp that's in the cupboard under the stairs?' she asked her mother.

'You never use those old motorbike parts that are in your garage,' she said to her uncle. 'Can I have some of them to help make my new bike?'

She asked other people in her family for different things too and soon the garden was full of pieces of metal and plastic. 'This is great,' she thought. 'I just need a second wheel now.'

What else do I need?

She decided to go and ask the new family in the flat on the third floor. Perhaps they could help her. She ran upstairs and knocked on the door.

'What do you want?' said the girl who opened it.

'Have you got an old bicycle wheel?' Ruby said. 'I need one so I can ride in the Under-12s race.'

'No, I haven't,' the girl said. (Her name was Victoria Rich.) 'But I'm going to win that race. My brilliant silver bicycle is the fastest bike in town. Now please go away. I'm playing the piano.' And Victoria Rich closed the door.

'Well!' thought Ruby. 'She wasn't very friendly!'

Ruby's grandfather phoned her that evening. Ruby told him about the unfriendly girl and about the wheel that she still needed. 'I'll come and see you tomorrow,' he said. 'I'll bring you a wheel and something else that will help. Don't worry! We'll make a brilliant bike for you too!'

'Here you are!' he said when he arrived with the wheel the next morning. 'And this spanner is for you. I've had it for 40 years. It's very special. It can fix anything!'

Ruby took the spanner carefully and turned it over and over in her hand. 'It's a brilliant present and I'll use it a lot, I'm sure,' she said quietly. 'Thanks, Grandpa!'

They started to work and they worked all day until the bike was ready.

Ruby stood up and looked at it. 'Wow! It's brilliant, Grandpa!' she laughed.

She went riding on her bike every morning and each time she rode it faster. Sometimes a metal or plastic piece fell off and Ruby had to stop, go back and fetch it. But Ruby always had the spanner in her pocket. It could fix any problem.

On the day of the race, Ruby and her family arrived at the starting line early. About 50 children from the town were already there. Ruby suddenly saw Victoria, who was sitting on her beautiful bike. She had a big smile on her face. Victoria looked at Ruby's bike and laughed. But Ruby's grandfather put his arm round Ruby's shoulder and whispered, 'Remember. Your bike is brilliant too!'

Then the race started. The first six kilometres round the lake were easy. The next five kilometres through the wood were more difficult and four of the children decided to stop. The next nine kilometres over the hills and past the farms were very hard work, and lots more children were too tired to cycle any more, but Ruby didn't stop. More and more children stopped and more and more parts of Ruby's bike fell off, but with her special spanner Ruby could fix anything.

When Ruby was only one kilometre from the end, Victoria was only about 20 metres in front of her. Ruby was very tired. 'I'm not going to stop. I'm going to finish this race. Victoria may win,' she thought, 'but my bike is brilliant too.'

Suddenly, a kangaroo hopped across the road just in front of them. Victoria nearly fell off because she was so surprised. Her back wheel started wobbling very badly, so she got off to look at it.

'Wow! I may win now!' Ruby thought when she raced past Victoria. But Victoria looked so angry and sad that Ruby turned her bike round and cycled back again.

'I can fix your bike with my special spanner!' Ruby said. 'It will only take a minute. Don't worry.'

'You're very kind,' Victoria said. 'I'm sorry for being so unfriendly. Perhaps we can both win this race!'

'That sounds like a great idea,' Ruby said and smiled. 'There! It's fine now.'

Victoria and Ruby got back on their brilliant bikes and cycled together to the finishing line. When they crossed it, Ruby waved the spanner in the air and her grandfather clapped and shouted, 'Well done!'

Well done!

'One day, Ruby,' he said, 'that special spanner is going to help you to make the fastest racing car in the world.'

'I know!' Ruby answered.

1 Brilliant bikes!

A New words for you!

Draw lines between the words and different parts of the picture.

| garage | wheel | fix | wobble | cycle |

B What happened next?

Write 2–7 in the boxes. Draw lines to show the right order.

1	Ruby finished making her brilliant bike.
	Ruby saw the poster about the race.
	Grandfather gave Ruby a wheel.
	Ruby made a toy racing car.
	Ruby and Victoria won the race.
	Ruby decided to make a bike.
	Victoria had problems with her bike.

C Who did this?

Write A, B or C.   A Ruby   B Ruby's grandfather   C Victoria Rich

1 ☐   2 ☐   3 ☐   4 ☐   5 ☐   6 ☐

Before the race

Complete the sentences. Write 1, 2, 3 or 4 words.

Example: In this story, ...Ruby............ is 11 years old.

1 Ruby's mum and dad never gave her .... for her birthday.

2 Ruby would like to be an ....

3 She wants to make .... in the world one day.

4 The poster about the race was on the wall outside the ....

5 .... was the date of the race.

6 People should .... Richard Black about the race.

 CD2 05 **Ruby finds out more about the race.**

Listen to Richard and Ruby. Tick the box.

1 What time does the race start?

      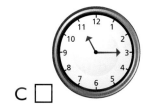

A ☐   B ☐   C ☐

2 What number must Ruby wear on her T-shirt?

A ☐   B ☐   C ☐

 It's too slow. It's not fast enough.

Write words in the spaces.

 Oh dear! I'm not brave enough to do that! And my bike's too old to do that!

Yes, Grandma, you're .... to do that! And your bike .... to do that!

G Can I have those old motorbike parts?

What does Ruby say to her uncle? Choose an answer A–H.

1 Uncle: Hello, Ruby! How are you?   Ruby: ...B...
2 Uncle: Why do you want them?   Ruby: ......
3 Uncle: Where are you making it?   Ruby: ......
4 Uncle: When did you start making it?   Ruby: ......
5 Uncle: Yes, you can have them, Ruby!   Ruby: ......

A Because I'm making a new bike. Mine isn't fast enough.
B I'm fine, thanks! Can I have those old motorbike parts?
C Two days ago. Will you give them to me?
D Thanks very much! Wow! They're heavy.
E No, I can't. See you later, Uncle!
F He's been here since Thursday.
G Great! Can I have them?
H In our garage.

H Find the differences.

**Look at the big picture on page 53 and at this picture.
Find 6 differences.**

What else
do I need?

I I may go for a bike ride.

Ask and answer questions.

'What will you do this afternoon?'
'I don't know. I may … or I may …'

Listen. Draw a line from the starting line to the finishing line!

K **Ruby's email**

Write the missing words and find Ruby's 3 spelling mistakes.

From:	Ruby@thebikefixer.au.org
To:	Danny
Date:	18 June 21:03
Subject:	The bike race

Hi! The bike race .....was..... amazing!

Victoria **(1)** .... I both won! Someone put a silver blanket round my shoulders at the end of the race. Someone else gave me a **(2)** .... of water. Then a journalist from the newspaper arrived. He asked me lots of questions about my bicycle. I was too excited to **(3)** .... all of them! He **(4)** .... some photos of it too. He may write a storey about it!

Grandpa was so happy. I love the spanner that he gave me. He's had it **(5)** .... fourty years! It can **(6)** .... anything! I may bring it to school to show you one day.

See **(7)** .... tommorrow!
Ruby

L **Play the game. Let's make these words!**

Harry was a cook. He worked in Graywalls Castle where he had to cook all the meals for Queen Alice. The queen was very unkind and she often made Harry's job very difficult. Harry and his two helpers, John and Karl, worked hard in the castle kitchen every day, but Queen Alice never gave them any money, so their families only ate cold vegetables. They were hungry and unhappy most of the time and Queen Alice was angry most of the time. Nothing could make her smile.

One day, she called Harry and said, 'I hate birthdays, but next Friday I will be 50 years old, so make a birthday cake for me. I want you to put 50 kinds of food in this cake and it must be the biggest and the best cake I have ever tasted. Do you understand?'

'Yes, I do,' Harry said, and went back downstairs to the kitchen to tell John and Karl the bad news.

John and Karl tried to think of things to put in the cake.

'We could put eggs, jam and lots of butter and milk in it,' John said.

'What else can we put in it?' Harry asked.

'We can put flour, mangoes and brown sugar in it too!' Karl said.

'OK. That's seven different things. What else?' Harry asked again.

'How about some lemon juice, apples, coffee, carrots and chocolate?' said a child who suddenly appeared in the kitchen. Harry didn't know her, but she looked kind and friendly.

'Thank you!' he said. 'Those are great ideas!'

Soon, they had 49 different kinds of food on the table. John and Karl began to mix everything together in an enormous bowl, but Harry stopped them. 'We've got a problem,' he said. 'We've only got 49 things to put in this cake but the queen wants 50! We need one more thing.'

The girl took a pear from her pocket and said, 'Here! This is from my grandmother's special pear tree. It'll make the cake taste really delicious!'

Harry took the little pear and added it to all the other food in the bowl.

'Thank you very much!' he said. 'Now, let's cook this cake!'

Harry, John and Karl carried the cake carefully to the old cooker. Then they went outside to work in the vegetable garden. The girl waved goodbye and disappeared into the wood that was next to the castle.

An hour later, Harry went back to look at the cake. But when he opened the kitchen door, he couldn't see the table, the cooker or the stairs that went up to the queen's dining room. The room was full of cake! He broke a piece off and ate it. 'Wow! This cake tastes fantastic!' he laughed. 'It's the biggest and the most delicious cake that I've ever made!'

The queen looked out of the top window. 'What's happening down there?' she called. 'And where's my birthday cake?'

'We've made it,' Harry answered, 'but it's so enormous we can't get back into the kitchen.'

'That means you can't bring me my dinner yet, and I didn't eat enough lunch, so I'm still hungry!' Queen Alice shouted angrily. 'Do something quickly!'

Harry looked at John and Karl. 'We must eat the cake,' he said, 'because we can't get back into the kitchen until we do!'

The three cooks began to eat the cake and each day the cake got more and more delicious and each day the three cooks got happier and happier. Their wives and children came to eat the cake too and soon all the people from the village came to help eat the cake. Everyone forgot their problems and started to smile again. The girl watched from the top of a tree in the wood and smiled too.

The people from the village were getting happier and happier, but Queen Alice was getting hungrier and hungrier and angrier and angrier. She could only eat dry biscuits and she could only drink rain water from the little gold cup that she left outside her window.

The cooks, their families and the people from the village finished eating the cake on the morning of the queen's birthday. Harry put the last piece on a beautiful silver plate and carried it carefully up the stairs. He didn't feel afraid of the queen now. He felt happy and brave.

'This is the most delicious piece of the cake and it's for you,' he said kindly.

Queen Alice looked at Harry, took the cake, ate it slowly and smiled at him. 'She's never, never, never done that before!' Harry thought. The queen smiled again. 'I can taste 49 kinds of food in this cake, but what's the last one? It tastes better than anything else in the world,' she said.

'It's a special pear,' Harry answered. 'A kind and happy little girl gave it to us to put in your cake.'

'Yes, I did,' the girl in the wood whispered. 'My grandmother's kindness and happiness are in your cake too. They were our present to you and to everyone in the village. Happy birthday, Your Majesty!'

8 A cake for the queen

A New words for you!

Draw lines between your new words and their meanings.

delicious   very good to eat

enormous   very

fantastic   different, better, more important

special   very big

really   great

B Who said this?

Write A, B or C.

A   B   C

Example:
Where's my birthday cake? ....C....

1
This cake tastes fantastic! ....

2
I hate birthdays. ....

3
What's happening down there? ....

4
Happy birthday, Your Majesty! ....

5
What else can we put in it?. ....

6
It'll make the cake taste really delicious. ....

C Right or wrong?

Write *right* or *wrong*.

Example: The three cooks were poor.   ....*right*....

1 The queen was always kind to the cooks.   ....

2 Harry knew the girl in the kitchen.   ....

3 The girl gave the cooks her grandmother's pear.   ....

4 There was a wood next to the castle.   ....

5 More than one person ate a piece of the cake.   ....

6 Harry was afraid when he took the cake to the queen. ....

What's happening in the kitchen?

Look at the picture on page 60. Write *yes* or *no*.

Example:
Three delicious biscuits are on a silver plate.
 no

1 You can see a chicken on the ground.
....

2 There is one large pocket on the girl's dress.
....

3 One of the cooks has burnt his finger!
....

4 Someone has opened the door of the old cooker.
....

5 There's an enormous spoon in Harry's right hand.
....

6 It's two o'clock in the afternoon.
....

What have they done?

Write the missing words in each sentence.

Example: Harry ...has broken... lots of eggs into the bowl.   (break)

1 John .... some milk in the bowl too.   (put)

2 They .... the coffee.   (add)

3 Another cook .... the chocolate.   (bring)

4 The girl .... the pear to Harry.   (give)

5 Harry .... all the food together.   (mix)

6 John and Karl .... the table!   (not clean)

65

F What kind of food is this?

Write the word.

Example: These are orange. They're vegetables.

c a r r o t s

1 This is white or brown. Some people put it in tea.

_ _ _ _ _

2 This yellow fruit isn't sweet.

_ _ _ _ _

3 This is white. You need it to make cakes and bread.

_ _ _ _ _

4 This drink comes from fruit or vegetables.

_ _ _ _ _

5 These orange fruits grow in hot countries.

_ _ _ _ _ _ _

6 This is usually dark brown and tastes sweet.

_ _ _ _ _ _ _ _

 ## G CD2 08 This tastes delicious!

Listen and write Robert's answers. Write one word.

Hello Robert! Let's talk about food.

What do you like eating for breakfast?

.........eggs.........

Who cooks the meals in your house?

....

Where do you eat your meals?

....

Tell me about the food you often eat.

I love ....

I often have .... for dinner.

I usually have .... on my bread.

H *yet* and *still*

Cross out the wrong word in each sentence.

Example: The queen is ~~yet~~/still sitting in her room.

1 Harry hasn't brought the queen her birthday cake yet/still.

2 The cooks are yet/still eating the cake.

3 The queen hasn't eaten her biscuits yet/still.

4 The cooks haven't eaten all the cake yet/still.

5 The queen is yet/still hungry and angry.

two days ago

now

Change part of the story.

Write new words in the spaces.

The cooks, their ......friends..... and the people from the village finished eating the cake on the morning of the queen's birthday. Harry put the last piece on a **(1)** .... silver plate and **(2)** .... it carefully up the stairs. He didn't feel afraid of the queen now. He felt happy and **(3)** .... 'This is the **(4)** .... piece of the cake and it's for you,' he said **(5)** ....

CD2 09 **Who's in the vegetable garden?**

Listen and draw lines.

Harry   John   Michael   Anna

Helen   Karl   Sarah   Richard

Who was the girl?

You decide. Write and say.

What was the girl's name?

How old was she?

Why did she want to help Queen Alice and everyone in the village?

What did she do next?

My friend!

Write about a friend.

Katy's favourite song

Some children don't like going to school very much. They prefer the holidays when they can have fun at home, visit exciting new places or perhaps go swimming at the beach or skiing in the mountains. But Katy and her friend Paul loved being at school.

Katy was great at maths and Paul was really good at English, but their favourite lesson was music. Paul had a guitar and could play it very well. Katy started to learn to play the piano when she was five, but she enjoyed singing more and she was very good at it. She dreamed of being a singer one day.

Their music teacher, Mr White, often brought CDs to the music lessons so the children could listen to different kinds of music from other countries. When the children liked a song a lot, Mr White wrote the words on the board. Then all the children sang the song together. Everyone loved Mr White's lessons.

Katy's favourite singer was called Alex Pepper. Katy loved watching him on TV. He was a brilliant dancer too and wore great clothes. Katy had all his CDs at home. She knew all the words to his songs and had posters of him on all the walls in her bedroom.

Paul loved Alex's songs too, and could play most of them on his guitar. Paul wanted to be the greatest guitar player in the world.

One day, Mr White said to the children, 'On Thursday next week, we're going to have a music competition here at school. If you want to be in the competition, you must sing or play a song. Alex Pepper is going to be in our town that day, so he's going to come to the school to listen to you all! He'll choose the winners and give them their prizes.'

'What are the prizes, Mr White?' Paul asked.

'Ten tickets to go and hear Alex Pepper sing!' Mr White answered.

Paul and Katy wanted to be in the competition, and they wanted to win, of course! They chose an easy song called 'I'll help you!'. They practised and practised at Katy's house every afternoon after school until it was Thursday. Katy's parrot liked listening and learnt all the words to the song too!

On the day of the competition, everyone was really excited. They all had to go into the school hall at two o'clock. Alex Pepper came in with the head teacher and everyone clapped. He was wearing a black jacket, black jeans and silver shoes and he was carrying a big red guitar.

'This is scary ...' thought Katy.

'Wow, what a brilliant guitar!' thought Paul.

Alex smiled and waved at everyone and then sat down between the head teacher and Mr White. Then the competition began. Lots of other children sang before Paul and Katy. One boy played his drums too loudly (the head teacher put his hands over his ears) and an older girl sang very well. Lots of children stood up to clap when she finished and shouted, 'More! More!'

'She's going to win,' thought Katy.

'You're next!' called Mr White, and pointed to Paul and Katy.

When Paul picked up his guitar and Katy saw all the people in the hall in front of them, she began to feel afraid. 'A thousand eyes are looking at me and I've forgotten all the words to the song that we've practised!' she whispered to Paul. 'I just can't remember them!'

'Katy,' Paul said quietly, 'you bought Alex's newest CD last week, didn't you? I can play all his songs. Which is your favourite?'

'The one that's called "I'm your friend", but it's really difficult to sing.'

'It's OK. I'll help you! We can sing it together,' Paul said.

Alex smiled at them and Katy began to feel better. Paul started to play and suddenly Katy forgot that she was in a school competition. She was in her dream of being a singer. She sang brilliantly and at the end of the song, Alex and some of the others stood up and clapped very loudly. 'That was excellent! Well done!' Alex shouted.

At the end of the competition, Alex Pepper and the head teacher and Mr White talked quietly together for a few minutes. Then Mr White stood up and said, 'Katy and Paul are the winners!'

The two friends jumped up and down. They were so surprised and so happy!

'You sang my favourite song,' Alex said to them.

'It's my favourite song too,' said Katy.

'Good!' said Alex. 'Well, here are your tickets. Who will come with you to hear me sing?'

'I'll invite my grandma,' laughed Katy. 'She really loves your music! But some of my friends will come with me too.'

Alex smiled. 'What about you, Paul?' he asked.

'Oh! I'll bring my best friend, Tony. He's the one who played the drums!' Paul answered. 'I'll invite my sisters too, I think!'

That evening when Katy arrived home, her parrot said, 'Hello, Katy! I'm your friend!'

Katy laughed. 'I'm your friend too! Do you know – today was very scary but fun, and very exciting too!'

But the day that she went to see Alex Pepper was the best, the most fun and the most exciting of her life!

Katy's favourite song

A New words for you!

Draw lines between your new words and the pictures.

poster

practise

scary

clap

prize

B Right or wrong?

Tick the right or wrong box.

	right	wrong
Example: Katy and Paul enjoyed school.	✔	☐
1 Paul played the guitar very well.	☐	☐
2 Mr White taught maths.	☐	☐
3 Alex Pepper was a famous singer.	☐	☐
4 Katy had a parrot that could speak.	☐	☐
5 The competition was at the town's sports centre.	☐	☐
6 Katy sang 'I'll help you!' in the competition.	☐	☐

C What happened next?

Write 2–6 in the stars. Draw lines to show the right order.

1   Alex Pepper gave the first prize to Katy and Paul.

Katy and her grandmother went to see Alex Pepper.

Katy and Paul practised very hard.

The parrot learnt all the words to 'I'll help you!'.

Mr White told the children about the competition.

Katy couldn't remember the words to a song.

D Katy and Paul

Complete the sentences. Write 2 or 3 words.

Example: When Katy began playing ....the piano.... she was only five.

1 Katy listened to music from .... in her music lessons.

2 The teacher sometimes .... to songs on the board.

3 Katy enjoyed watching a singer called .... on TV.

4 Paul wanted to be the best .... in the world.

5 The .... was on Thursday.

6 Katy and Paul practised a song called '.........................'.

E We're going to see Alex Pepper!

What are Katy, Paul and their friends going to do next Thursday? Complete the speech bubbles. Use words from the box.

take   invite   wait   ~~ask~~   wear   sit

Example:
I'm ...going to ask... him to write his name on my CD!

1
I'm .... my new jacket!

2
I'm .... him to my party!

3
I'm .... next to him in the school hall.

4
I'm .... lots of pictures of him.

5
I'm .... for him outside so I can walk into school with him!

F Now let's talk about clothes ...

Match the clothes and the words. Draw lines.

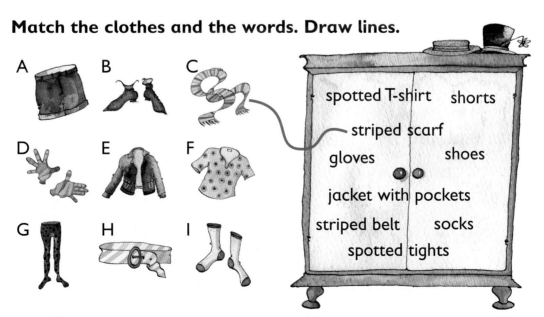

A   B   C

spotted T-shirt   shorts

striped scarf

gloves   shoes

D   E   F

jacket with pockets

striped belt   socks

G   H   I

spotted tights

What are Katy and Paul wearing?

Listen and colour and write in the picture on page 70.

 Alex Pepper's diary

Listen and write.

Go to music competition!

Example: Day .....Thursday.....

1 Music competition is at .... School

2 Leave home at: ....

3 Wear: black jacket, black jeans and ....

4 Take: .... and ten tickets

5 Mr White's phone number: ....

 I'll take some CDs.

What will you do for the party? Talk and write.

A party? Great! I'll make some cakes.

I'll take some CDs.

CD2 13 Katy's favourite song

Listen and write.

I'm your friend.

1 I'm your friend,
So call my name
If you want to play
I'll stay all .... !

2 When you feel
....
Don't be alone.
If you want a friend,
Just ring my phone.

3 I'm your friend,
So come to me
If you want to talk
Or go for a .... !

4 When you feel
....
Don't be alone.
If you want a friend,
Just ring my phone.

5 We're your friends,
So call our names.
We'll bring our
smiles
And all our ....

When do you like being alone? When do you like being with friends?

 Katy's sister's guitar lesson

Choose a word to put in each space.

I had my first guitar lesson today. My music teacher's ...name.. is Mr
Quick. First I had to learn **(1)** .... hold the guitar. That was
difficult **(2)** .... my new guitar is big and heavy, but
I had lots **(3)** .... fun! I want to learn quickly and
play very well like Paul.
After my lesson I **(4)** .... home on my bike. After
dinner, I played my guitar again! I practised until I
went to bed. I played very loudly! Katy loved it but
Mum said, 'I'm happy that you **(5)** .... going to learn
to play the guitar and not the drums!' I'm **(6)** .... to have
another guitar lesson tomorrow!

 We like competitions!

Make a poster for another competition at school.

William's strangest story

William hated getting up in the mornings! He loved lying in his warm bed and thinking about flying in space rockets or finding dinosaurs. That was much more interesting than getting ready for school. He was late for school nearly every day but he enjoyed thinking of stories to tell his teacher, too.

'I'm late because our dog ate my maths homework, so I had to do that again before I had my breakfast, and my little sister threw my school uniform in the bath. Mum had to dry it before I could put it on, and someone stole Dad's car at midnight last night, so I had to walk all the way here!'

Of course, the teacher didn't believe William's stories, but the other children in the class loved them. 'You might win a writing competition one day!' his best friend said. 'You might write a story book one day. You might be famous!' the others said.

One morning, William lay in bed thinking about visiting other planets. When he turned on his mobile phone and saw the time, he thought, 'Oh no! I'm going to be late again!'

He jumped out of bed and started getting dressed. Then he remembered something important. He had to take a dictionary, a pair of scissors, some glue and a ball of wool to school. He needed these for his English, art, geography and science lessons that day.

He found them, but it was already two minutes to nine when he left the house. His lessons started at nine o'clock, so he had to run very fast.

He ran so fast that he fell over and hit his head on the ground. When he opened his eyes, he wasn't in the street by the school playground. He was sitting in a spaceship and a space monster was laughing and pointing its long fingers at him.

'Well,' thought William, 'today I'm going to be *really* late for school!'

'||^*@@^>>,' the space monster said. William didn't understand, but the monster was pointing at William's rucksack, so William opened it. His dictionary fell out. The space monster hopped over, picked it up, smelt it and then ate it! 'That tasted delicious!' it said.

'Wow!' thought William. 'That's fantastic! Now it can speak English. When I get home, I'm going to eat my Spanish dictionary!'

'What else have you got in your rucksack, Earth Boy?' the space monster asked.

William showed it the scissors. The space monster touched them carefully with its long fingers. 'What do you use these for?' it asked.

William looked for something that he could cut. He saw a square piece of gold and silver paper next to the spaceship's computer. It had lots of stripes and spots on it.

'For cutting,' William said, and started cutting the paper in half. The spaceship suddenly stopped moving.

No! Stop!

'No! Stop! That was my most important space map!' the space monster said angrily.

'Wow!' thought William. 'I've got a really big problem now. Without a map, it might take much more time to get to school!'

Then the space monster saw William's glue and ball of wool. It picked them up but the glue fell through its fingers and dropped on the floor. The top came off and the glue came out. It went all over the space monster's feet.

'Do you drink this or wash in it?' the space monster asked.

'Jump in it and see!' William answered.

The monster jumped into the glue and tried to jump out again but it couldn't. It threw the ball of wool in the air, and when it started waving its arms round and round, the wool went round and round its arms too. Soon the monster couldn't move at all.

Go home!

'^^&%'> my ship!' it shouted. (It was forgetting its English words.) 'I've got a horrible headache because I'm >^((* your strange language. You've broken my space ^^<* and now I can't move my *)>/! or my arms! I'm sending you home! Go home right now!'

William was suddenly on the ground outside the empty school playground. It was five past nine. He ran into his classroom and said, 'I'm sorry I'm late. You see, I was in a spaceship and I couldn't get away. A space monster ate my dictionary. Then I cut up the space map, so the spaceship couldn't move. Then I glued the space monster's feet to the floor and my wool went all round its arms, which made it really angry. But everything's OK now!'

His friends couldn't stop laughing.

'Well,' the teacher said. 'William, that's the strangest story you've ever told me. I don't believe any of it!'

William smiled and looked inside his empty rucksack. 'Well, I know all of it *really* happened,' he laughed.

10 William's strangest story

A New words for you!

Write a word under each picture.

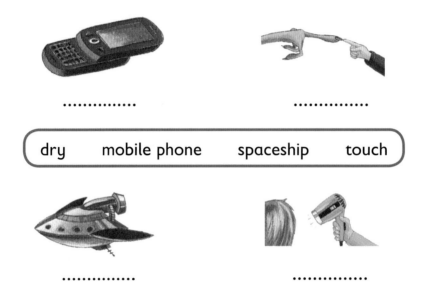

....

dry   mobile phone   spaceship   touch

....

B Can you remember?

Cross out the wrong word in each sentence.

Example: William was late/early for school nearly every day.

1 The children in William's class hated/loved his stories.

2 William took some glue/paper to school with him that day.

3 The space monster read/ate William's English dictionary.

4 William cut up a map/newspaper with his scissors.

5 At the end of the story, the space monster was angry/hungry.

C CD2 15 Who's talking about this story?

Listen and tick the right box.

Fred ☐   Helen ☐   Peter ☐

D I'm late again because ...

Choose different words to complete William's story.

I'm late because a .....goat..... ate my (1) ....
homework, so I had to do that again before I ate my

(2) .... Then my little sister threw my school

(3) .... in the bath. (4) .... had to dry

it before I could put it on, and someone stole Dad's

(5) .... at midnight last night, so I had to

(6) .... to school this morning.

breakfast
thanked
bin
shirt
Grandma
run
spent
~~goat~~
geography
motorbike

E I might see a spaceship!

'What might happen tomorrow?'
'I don't know. I might ... A space monster might ...'

F ⊙CD2 16 What must William take to each lesson?

Listen and write a letter in each box.

English	D
geography	☐
maths	☐
music	☐
science	☐
history	☐

A   B   C   D

E   F   G

Find the differences.

Look at the first picture on page 78 and at this picture.
Find 6 differences.

 What do you like doing?

Tell the others in your class.

What do you like doing? What do you enjoy reading?

What do you love eating? What do you hate doing?

Did William do this?

Choose a word for each space.

> for   on   off   off   over   ~~up~~   up

Example: William didn't like getting ...up... in the morning.

1 William turned .... his mobile phone to see the time.

2 William fell .... near the school playground.

3 William took .... his shoes and put them in the spaceship.

4 William cut .... the space map.

5 William turned .... the computer in the spaceship.

6 William looked .... something that could help the space monster.

J William's diary

Write the missing words and find 3 spelling mistakes!

Monday

I didn't ......*get*...... up until 8.15 this morning because I was thinking about (1) .... to another planet. I might do that one day. I ran all the way to school, but then I fell (2) .... and hurt my head. I couldn't beleive the next thing that happened. I was in a spaceship and I couldn't get away. A crazy space monster ate my dictonary. Then I cut up his space map. The spaceship couldn't move after that. I got angry then becose I wanted (3) .... get to school, so I told the space monster to stand in some glue! It couldn't move. It got angry too then and my wool went all round its arms. It sent me home after that!

My friends laughed (4) .... my story, but I know it happened! I'm going to write a longer story on my computer (5) .... meeting the monster. I (6) .... writing stories. I might write a book one day!

K Why were you late today?

Complete the sentences.

I'm sorry I'm late!

I ....

Then my ....

and after that, ...

L Play the game. What do you use this for?

You're talking to the space monster. It's got some questions for you!

1

2

3

4

Unit word list

1 Ben's wishes

nouns

Africa ....

chocolate ....

fire ....

gorilla ....

group ....

hole ....

insect ....

minute ....

money ....

sky ....

sweets ....

way ....

winter ....

wish ....

wool ....

world ....

adjectives

dangerous ....

empty ....

full ....

gold ....

important ....

kind ....

lovely ....

lucky ....

poor ....

same ....

silver ....

soft ....

warm ....

verbs

appear ....

believe ....

belong ....

break ....

dig ....

disappear ....

fall ....

feel ....

fight ....

find out ....

look after ....

spend (time) ....

use ....

visit ....

wish ....

adverbs

anywhere ....

enough ....

everywhere ....

hard ....

nowhere ....

perhaps ....

really ....

somewhere ....

suddenly ....

usually ....

expressions

Don't be silly! ....

② The glove, the fork and the old pair of glasses

nouns

butterfly ....

crab ....

finger ....

flag ....

fork ....

glove ....

hook ....

pair ....

problem ....

ring ....

rucksack ....

ship ....

swing ....

volleyball ....

wing ....

adjectives

bored ....

dangerous ....

deep ....

full ....

gold ....

lovely ....

salty ....

silver ....

silly ....

unhappy ....

verbs

arrive ....

believe ....

bite ....

could ....

hook ....

might ....

pull ....

sound (like) ....

whisper ....

will ....

adverbs

perhaps ....

suddenly ....

prepositions

away ....

through ....

pronouns

no-one ....

expressions

Excellent! ....

Of course ....

Robert and the three envelopes

nouns

bank ....

beak ....

bridge ....

building ....

chemist ....

envelope ....

factory ....

hill ....

hotel ....

job ....

letter ....

London ....

message ....

middle ....

minute ....

money ....

paper ....

piece ....

pocket ....

police station ....

postcard ....

post office ....

programme ....

secret ....

shelf ....

ship ....

sky ....

station ....

summer ....

time ....

world ....

year ....

adjectives

busy ....

enough ....

excited ....

fast ....

friendly ....

heavy ....

high ....

same ....

strange ....

wonderful ....

verbs

fall ....

finish ....

happen ....

remember ....

spend (time) ....

thank ....

travel ....

adverbs

ago ....

away ....

tomorrow ....

prepositions

across ....

past ....

through ....

until ....

pronouns

someone ....

expressions

Hi! ....

See you soon! ....

(4) Lara and the mountain lion

nouns

cave ....

handkerchief ....

hour ....

medicine ....

minute ....

pocket ....

rucksack ....

spoon ....

time ....

vet ....

winter ....

world ....

year ....

adjectives

brave ....

dark ....

furry ....

high ....

horrible ....

little ....

other ....

plastic ....

sick ....

soft ....

strange ....

unkind ....

wonderful ....

verbs

arrive ....

become ....

believe ....

comb ....

decide ....

disappear ....

feel ....

finish ....

happen ....

hear ....

look after ....

ski ....

stay ....

turn ....

adverbs

after ....

before ....

enough ....

ever ....

fast ....

just ....

kindly ....

next ....

soon ....

suddenly ....

prepositions

for (time) ....

without ....

expressions

No problem! ....

See you later! ....

Sure! ....

⑤ Big Nose and the Storm-Maker

nouns

air ....

drum ....

handkerchief ....

hill ....

husband ....

ice ....

knife ....

lightning ....

news ....

octopus ....

problem ....

sky ....

smell ....

sound ....

spoon ....

storm ....

thunder ....

umbrella ....

wave ....

wife ....

world ....

adjectives

dangerous ....

east ....

enormous ....

foggy ....

frightening ....

north ....

real ....

scared ....

south ....

true ....

unhappy ....

warm ....

west ....

verbs

begin ....

blow ....

brush ....

change ....

cut ....

disappear ....

happen ....

may ....

mix ....

sell ....

shiver ....

should ....

smell ....

sound (like) ....

turn ....

whistle ....

wish ....

worry ....

adverbs

soon ....

still ....

suddenly ....

pronouns

no-one ....

expressions

Thank you so much! ....

⑥ Michael and the red rug

nouns

April ....

belt ....

classmate ....

corner ....

cushion ....

date ....

fun ....

future ....

half ....

internet ....

key ....

kilometre ....

March ....

midday ....

middle ....

midnight ....

minute ....

month ....

north ....

phone call ....

player ....

pocket ....

pool party ....

poster ....

quarter ....

rucksack ....

rug ....

team ....

volleyball ....

adjectives

dizzy ....

empty ....

excited ....

front ....

full ....

interesting ....

lovely ....

strange ....

unhappy ....

warm ....

verbs

arrive ....

begin ....

believe ....

change ....

decide ....

feel ....

happen ....

hear ....

ring (phone) ....

smell ....

sound (like) ....

speak ....

stay ....

turn ....

adverbs

away ....

even ....

fast ....

somewhere ....

soon ....

suddenly ....

expressions

How are you doing? ....

Sure! ....

What's the time? ....

(7) **Brilliant bikes!**

nouns

bicycle ....

engineer ....

fire station ....

garage ....

glue ....

journalist ....

June ....

kilometre ....

metal ....

month ....

newspaper ....

plastic ....

pocket ....

poster ....

problem ....

race ....

scissors ....

spanner ....

wheel ....

wood ....

adjectives

brilliant ....

excited ....

fast ....

friendly ....

hard ....

ready ....

silver ....

special ....

sure ....

verbs

arrive ....

clap ....

cycle ....

decide ....

fall off ....

fetch ....

fix ....

knock ....

may ....

race ....

sound (like) ....

take (time) ....

whisper ....

win ....

wobble ....

worry ....

adverbs

ago ....

already ....

early ....

enough ....

nearly ....

suddenly ....

tomorrow ....

prepositions

for (time) ....

past ....

since ....

(8) A cake for the queen

nouns

biscuit ....

castle ....

chocolate ....

cook ....

cooker ....

fire ....

flour ....

fork ....

hour ....

meal ....

money ....

news ....

piece ....

plate ....

pocket ....

problem ....

queen ....

spoon ....

sugar ....

wife ....

wood ....

adjectives

brave ....

delicious ....

enormous ....

fantastic ....

friendly ....

full ....

gold ....

kind ....

poor ....

silver ....

special ....

unhappy ....

unkind ....

verbs

appear ....

break ....

burn ....

could ....

disappear ....

forget ....

happen ....

hate ....

hear ....

mix ....

taste ....

whisper ....

adverbs

before ....

ever ....

hard ....

later ....

still ....

yet ....

prepositions

into ....

until ....

pronouns

anything ....

everyone ....

expressions

What else? ....

⑨ Katy's favourite song

nouns

belt ....

competition ....

dancer ....

drum ....

English ....

fun ....

glove ....

maths ....

minute ....

poster ....

prize ....

shorts ....

thousand ....

tights ....

winner ....

adjectives

alone ....

brilliant ....

excellent ....

excited ....

other ....

scary ....

spotted ....

striped ....

verbs

clap ....

feel ....

finish ....

forget ....

practise ....

prefer ....

remember ....

ski ....

use ....

win ....

adverbs

o'clock ....

perhaps ....

suddenly ....

together ....

expressions

Of course ....

10 William's strangest story

nouns

art ....

bin ....

chopstick ....

comb ....

competition ....

dictionary ....

dinosaur ....

English ....

finger ....

geography ....

glue ....

half ....

history ....

language ....

maths ....

midnight ....

mobile ....

planet ....

rocket ....

rucksack ....

salt ....

science ....

scissors ....

ship ....

space ....

spaceship ....

spot ....

stamp ....

stripe ....

torch ....

uniform ....

way ....

wool ....

adjectives

empty ....

fantastic ....

important ....

interesting ....

other ....

Spanish ....

verbs

believe ....

break ....

comb ....

cut up ....

dry ....

fall over ....

glue ....

hate ....

leave ....

lie ....

send ....

smell ....

steal ....

taste ....

touch ....

turn off ....

turn on ....

visit ....

win ....

adverbs

already ....

angrily ....

nearly ....

really ....

suddenly ....

prepositions

through ....

without ....

pronouns

others ....

expressions

right now ....

Everything's OK now. ....

Drawings by some children who read this book

Katy's favourite song by Faye, age 7

A cake for the queen by Amber, age 7

Lara and the mountain lion by Faye, age 7

Big nose and the Storm-maker by Ryan, age 7

Acknowledgements

The author and publishers would like to thank the ELT professionals who commented on the material at different stages of its development:

Sean Fox and Rupert Procter, ABC Pathways School (Hong Kong); Jonathan Gibbons (Spain); Celia Gasgil (Turkey); Rosalie Kerr and Natasha Colbridge (UK)

The author and publishers would also like to thank Kathy Whiting and the children in Class 6 (Year 3 in 2009) at Arbury Primary School, Cambridge, for their insights and comments which helped us in developing the stories. Thanks are also due to all the children of members of staff at Cambridge University Press for reading and reviewing the stories.

The author is grateful to Niki Donnelly, Laila Friese and Jo Hunter of Cambridge University Press, and to Brigit Viney.

The author would like to thank Frances, Felicity, Helen and other colleagues she has worked with for the pure enjoyment of producing YLE material. Thanks are also given for a conversation in Ireland four years ago that prompted her to pen the first draft of the *Storyfun* units. On a personal note, Karen would also like to thank her mother and grandfather for the joy of being read stories as a child, and her sons, Tom and Will, for bringing so much creative fun to the continuation of the family storytelling tradition.

Editorial work by Brigit Viney

Cover design by Andrew Oliver

Cover illustration by Galia Bernstein (NB Illustration)

Book design and page make-up by eMC Design Ltd.

The author and publishers are grateful to the following illustrators:
Unit 1 Ben's wishes: Roland Dry (Beehive Illustration)
Unit 2 The glove, the fork and the old pair of glasses: Sarah Warburton
Unit 3 Robert and the three envelopes: Mark Beech (NB Illustration)
Unit 4 Lara and the mountain lion: Galia Bernstein (NB Illustration)
Unit 5 Big Nose and the Storm-Maker: Roland Dry (Beehive Illustration)
Unit 6 Michael and the red rug: Galia Bernstein (NB Illustration)
Unit 7 Brilliant bikes!: Sarah Warburton
Unit 8 A cake for the queen: Sophie Allsopp
Unit 9 Katy's favourite song: Harriet Stanes (NB Illustration)
Unit 10 William's strangest story: Mandy Field (Phosphor Art)

Sound recordings by John Green at TEFL Audio, London